T0209378

— THE —
WORKING
MAN

Matthew Melchezidek Ezekiel

WESTBOW
P R E S S®
A DIVISION OF THOMAS NELSON
& ZONDERVAN

WestBow Press books may be ordered through booksellers or by contacting:

WestBow Press
A Division of Thomas Nelson & Zondervan
1663 Liberty Drive
Bloomington, IN 47403
www.westbowpress.com
1 (866) 928-1240

Because of the dynamic nature of the Internet, any web addresses or
links contained in this book may have changed since publication and
may no longer be valid. The views expressed in this work are solely those
of the author and do not necessarily reflect the views of the publisher,
and the publisher hereby disclaims any responsibility for them.

Any people depicted in stock imagery provided by Getty Images are models,
and such images are being used for illustrative purposes only.
Certain stock imagery © Getty Images.

ISBN: 978-1-9736-8547-0 (sc)
ISBN: 978-1-9736-8548-7 (e)

Print information available on the last page.

WestBow Press rev. date: 2/18/2020

On or about February 14, 1990, I was arrested for 5 counts of arson. Two of the counts were aggravated arson which carries a mandatory 5 year sentence each. I woke up that morning on the date listed above and it was like any other morning or most mornings. I simply went to work. I think the weather was partly cloudly to clear and I was building a garage in the back yard of a customer I had in the east of Sodom City. I think it was about a little after lunch and my fiancee at that time gave me a call and said the police were looking for me because of my properties that had burned down or blew up in recent months prior. So, I said ok, and stopped work immediately went to the Sodom City police station, Central Station by A Street and B Street. When I got to the police station, I walked in and told a police officer who was working at a front desk a couple of police officers are looking for me. He asked me for my I.D. and I gave it to him. He looked up my name on his computer and then made a phone call to the officers who were looking for me.

He then told me to have a seat and they are on their way. Well, I guess 10 or 15 minutes went by and they showed up. One of the officers spoke and said, "Get up Jack Ace! You are under arrest." When he said that I knew to keep my mouth shut because I knew I had the right to remain silent. However, the strange thing here was, I was never asked any questions during the entire interrogation. They did all the talking and moving me around.

What had happened in the interrogation room was very traumatic and intense, but I will discussed this later on because I want to discuss what had happened to 4 of my properties and a neighbor's property 6 or 7 months prior to my arrest. I had several rental properties that I owned all around SODOM CITY. The first property, on Banana Street was a triplex. It blew up from a gas leak. The house was totaled. It had to be completely removed. After further research and investigation, it had been reported to the local utility company, ABC PUBLIC SERVICE INC, that there had been underground gas leaks and gas smells coming out from the house two to four months prior to the explosion. ABC PUBLIC SERVICE. had supposedly even repaired a leak in front of my house on Banana Street several months prior to the explosion. So with the neighbors account of smelling gas prior to the explosion and already file reports of gas leaks and gas smells it was quite obvious that ABC PUBLIC SERVICE had been neglectful in restoring the gas system to good working condition on my house on

BANANA Street. Next, a few streets over from the house on BANANA STREET, I had a duplex that burned down to the ground a couple or few weeks later. This place was located on APPLE Street. I had just finished renovating it to like brand new condition and no one could tell me what caused that fire. No fire investigator, no fire inspector, no insurance man, no one. An insurance man took samples of some charred debris, but couldn't determine nothing in his laboratory analogy of it. Third, I had a house on ELECTRIC Blvd on the lake which is on the other side of town in the east part of SODOM CITY.

Well, after a few months after my house on APPLE Street had burned down, my next door neighbor's house located on ELECTRIC Blvd had burned down. It was really weird. So weird, I started to get scared. My fiancee kept asking me what was going on and I would say "I DON'T KNOW!" Two of my properties were totally gone and now my neighbor's house is gone. She would joke and say, "maybe your workers are doing it!" I said" I don't think so." I didn't know what to think!!!Next, about 2 or 3 weeks later, now my house on the lake on ELECTRIC Blvd burns down. Now I was really scared. WHAT IN THE WORLD was going on? Is someone doing this to me?! If so, WHY?! Did I MAKE SOMEONE ANGRY?! Who could it be?! or maybe, they were ANGRY at my dad and taking it out on me. I was seriously confused and very frightened. Last, there was a 4-plex I helped to buy for my long-time worker of mine. His name is/was Joe Smith. I told him I'm buying this place for him and his family. (him, mother, and sister). You can rent out three units and that will pay for the mortgage note and plus you can make a little profit. You and your family can live in one unit comfortably. He was very happy.

Then one night the place supposedly catches fire, but not burned down, only a little damaged. This is where the police say they have all kinds of evidence. I was asking my lawyer at that time, where is all this evidence that they say they have. My lawyer told me they will present it later, but to this day, I NEVER SAW THIS EVIDENCE!!!!! The police were at this crime scene, the four-plex on ORANGE Street where I was helping my worker to buy, and my worker met them there. When my worker met them there, they immediately arrest him. My worker told me they were screaming at him and hitting him as he was put into the police car. He said he had URINATED on himself a little because he was so scarred. When they got to the police station interrogation room, Joe Smith told me they were still hitting him and knocking him around the room. They were saying things like "We are going to burn Jack Ace and we know you and him had a plan to make some money off insurance companies." He said "NO" and they hit him again. He said all he could do was just crouch down or bow his head a little and put his hand in front of his head and take it. Joe Smith also said they told him "A bunch of us are going to put Jack Ace away and you are going to help us. Joe Smith told me at that time, all he could do was just agree and do whatever they asked or told him to do. Then Joe Smith said they told him "We are going to type up a confession and you are going to sign it and if you don't, the F.B.I. are waiting across the street and they will be much rougher than us. You really don't want the feds in here. Then Joe Smith said, "ok, I'll sign it" After they typed it up, my worker, Joe Smith signed it. The officers smiled and said, "now we can go get Jack Ace."

So I guess with that signed confession, they had the authority to arrest me on the spot. Another maybe highly circumstancial or suspect detail surrounding these events is I acquired another or new identity because I had went bankrupct. A bankruptcy is on your record for 6 six years, so it's hard to get credit or get loans with a bankruptcy on your credit report. I found this book in a book store and the title of it was "How To Create A New Identity." So with this book I was able to obtain a new Identity which was David Bunn. With my new identity, I started operating my business. I wasn't hiding it. I was filing public papers under my new identity. I was in fact trying to make a new start, a clean slate. So in short, I was or am in fact both identities. If anyone were to ask me at any time if I was both people, I would have said "Yes". So I was the mortgage holder as David Bunn for my worker, Joe Smith's 4-plex property on ORANGE Street. Anyone can go to the municipal building where they record mortgages and get a copy to verify this fact. So, with this forced confession, the police officers were able to persue me full force and that is when they went to my fiancee's to see if I was there. That is when she called me when they left her. She told me they scared her because they were screaming at her. ok, now they have left her. She called me and I immediately stop work and went to the police station. ok, now we are back to the beginning of the story where I was waiting for the officers in the Central Police Station waiting room. They walked to the area where I was sitting and one officer stated, "Get up Jack Ace you are under arrest." As we were walking into some room, one officer sat behind a desk and started typing. The other officer kept standing me up and taking me to another small room and then back to the room where the officer was typing. He did this about 6 or 7 times running his mouth with **all** kinds of THINGS. The officer that was typing said to me "you must be some kind of Robin Hood." The other officer chuckled a little and said "Yep, he's a AFRO AMERICAN lover" Well, the officer who **WAS;** typing keeps typing and once again the other officer picks me up and takes me to another room running his mouth saying things like, "we got all the insurance companies, ABC PUBLIC SERVICE, the D.A. and **the** newspeople. We got everybody. You don't have a shot. You are not going to see the streets for a long time. We are going to burn you and all your properties, you AFRICAN AMERICAN lover." He chuckles a little and again he stands me up and walks me back into the room where the other officer is typing and sits me down. This time he leaves the room for a little while, so I'm in the room alone with the officer typing. The officer typing stops typing and looks at me and says "If you don't sign this form, you will be sorry." And he touches his gun. I was terrified. He then hands over a form with a pen and I sign it immediately. Another thing that was very strange and I really don't understand. I thought that if the F.B.I. is involved in an investigation of any sort they have to be present at every part of the investigation. They weren't present at my interrogation and they were involved in a plan to wait across the street at my worker's interrogation, so the local police can beat, hit, knock him around, and intimidate my worker into signing a phony confession. And if by some chance my worker was to endure all this and still hold his ground to the truth, they made sure they said, "If you think we are rough, the F.B.I. guys are waiting across the street and they are much worse than us." That would be the icing on the cake as the ultimate necessary and final intimidation needed to get him to sign the phony confession. My worker was traumatized and probably still is today. So after a few more times'them calling me a AFRICAN AMERICAN Lover and a Robin Hood, the officer who was typing stopped typing and they both took me out of the interrogation room and down a stairwell to go to jail. In the stairwell, one office says out loud, "Big Bill and Bad Bob oughta be happy now" and he smiles. The other office replied, "Don't worry about it. We did our part. Let's just take him to jail." So as we go out a door into the parking lot or garage, three news broadcast reporters were waiting with their cameras and bright lights. So as we, me and an officer on each side of me were walking towards the jail, these three reporters were running all around us filming us, me and the officers. As they were filming and running, they were giggling and laughing saying "Looks like we got a Robin Hood." Then another reporter stated, "Nah! He's an AFRO AMERICAN lover." Last, the third reporter stated, "He's an ;AFRO AMERICAN lover and a Robin Hood." All I could do was just put my hand-cuffed hands in front of my face and try to bow my head as much as I could hoping and praying no one would recognize me all over TV world.

This nightmare was getting worse and worse. Soo horrible. I was petrified. Ok. now I was in jail and waiting for my fiancee to bond me out somehow. My charges were 5 counts of arson and 2 of the counts were "aggravated arson" which carries a mandatory of 5 years each. So my fiancee had a friend who was friends with many politicians and wealthy men. So my fiancee calls this person and somehow they get me out. I was released and my fiancee and I went home. This was about February 14, 1990. So many thoughts and fears were going through my head. My first thought was I thought my fiancée was going to leave me. What all that had happened had been so "DISASTEROUS with me all over the news. My name was completely MUD now. To my great surprise, she didn't leave me. She stayed. I think she really loved me because most people would have bolted out immediately. So I go to work the next day feeling like I'm some kind of Hitler or some other crazy notorious guy hoping I don't or didn't get noticed after all that news coverage. Well, I go back to work at that same job where I was building a garage in the back yard of a customer located in the east of SODOM CITY. I started work some time in the early morning hours.

Then AFTER about an hour the customer comes out her back door and asks me if I could take a look at something in her bathroom. So I followed her into the house and we passed through her kitchen. She had a shotgun laying on her kitchen table. I just knew she put that there for me to see to give me some type of' MESSAGE like "Don't mess with me." So I guess that was my confirmation that she saw me all over the news. My heart just sanked. I guess that was when I first thought that Ineeded to get out of this town, my birthtown. I have now been so destroyed by the news, I don't think I could ever recover from this, An Absolute Horrible Feeling. I have a very religious up-bringing and I knew I needed to run to the "Mercy Seat." Well I finished the job and I never heard back again from that customer. She was a regular customer of my Dad's, so we have been doing business with her for a long time. So as time went on, we started getting calls from my fiancee's friend who had helped bond me out of jail. He started inviting my fiancee to parties at a boathouse where many politicians and wealthy men would attend. We thought that with all the charges I was facing and the idea I could go to jail for the rest of my life, we had to do what-ever it took to keep this person happy.

So my fiancee would go to these parties where she became friends -WITH these wealthy men and politicians at that time. So I guess you could say that these men were the most powerful men in Louisiana at that time. There were many parties at this boathouse and they would frequently go to other restaurants in the downtown area and have parties there as well. There were times my fiancee would become aggravated with all this. She was at one time going to these parties 3 or 4 times a week. She would sometimes say, "I want to stay home. I don't want to go around those. "PEOPLE" Yet, she would still go for me and us. In addition to all this, there was a time when they were taking her to bad bars. When I say bad bars, just use your imagination. It was terrible and all I could do was fall on my knees screaming to God. Also, a very important detail or aspect that needs to be noticed is that my fiancee had a modeling agency where she had 40 of the most beautiful girls in Sodom City working for her. Also, my fiancée was the most beautiful redhead in the entire city of SODOM. I'm not being biased because she's my fiancée. I have pictures to prove IT. When one looks at her pictures, one would agree hands down that she is/was the best. So one can see why these politicians and wealthy men wanted her and her models over at these parties. So during the course of all these things happening, my fiancee's friend who helped bond me out of jail gets my fiancee off to the side and tells her, "Don't worry about your boyfriend's charges. Everything is going to work out. We have everything under control and it's going to be alright. He's not going to jail. Just wait and you'll see everything will work out." We were like "FINALLY." We were like had a big sigh of relief because this thing was like going into two years.

In the meantime, my case just kept getting continued every month. The judge offered me a plea deal to plea guilty to all the charges and all I will receive were probation and community service. I said no. I was not pleading guilty to something I didn't do. Besides, I now have the most powerful people in SODOM on my side and they would get to the bottom of this and realize this whole thing was a set-up and find the true culprits or guilty ones. Hey, I had Tom Jackson. He was the number one head District Attorney of Sodom City at that time. He was one of the most admired man of integrity and character, a symbol of true righteousness and justice. So if there was an assistant District Attorney OR some sort of underling attorney working for Tom Jackson that was involved in framing me, Tom Jackson would find them and exposed them and all the other involved parties or people and bring all these people to justice. However, at the end of this book, he proved to be the most under-handed, double dealing, back-stabbing, deceitful, person. WHEELING DEALING AND STEALING WITHOUT FEELING. THERE IS TRULY A SPECIAL SPECIAL SPECIAL PLACE GOD HAS WAITING FOR HIM, 25 DEGREES HOTTER. A low down dirty snake in the grass.

SO As time went on, my case was still at a standstill. My case just kept being continued every month, every month, every month. I noticed two things happening while my case was being continued. One, my work had stopped, completely stopped. None of my old customers were calling me and I couldn't get any new work. It was like I had zero jobs. I advertise in newspapers, internet, and passed out flyers. Still no work. So it was like I was a bum doing nothing. Second, the pressure on my FIANCEE was extremely turned up. The way this happened was all of a sudden, all the girls that worked for my FIANCEE started making problems on the job thereby causing stress on my fiancee. Not only the girls causing problems, her clients were doing the same to her. They would make or create problems that my fiancee would have to deal with over and above the problems her girls were causing. Dealing with this all the time makes you stressful and exhausted and causes physical problems. When I say problems, it got so bad and ridiculous, then I realized here or at this point, there's got to be a third party involved making all this happen. Here, I am not having any work looking like a bum and she's about to pull her hair out of her head. Then I realize they were trying split us up by maybe making me look like a worthless bum in her eyes thereby making her to lose the love she has for me and she ends our relationship. So I decided because I wasn't doing nothing and can't get any work, I would do anything I could to help her. so I did. Any possible way 'that I could to help her I did it. I would run errands for her, I would cook, clean, sew, and renovate the house. I would be a chauffer for her girls. I would do anything and everything I could to try to ease or take some of the stress away from her. I would cook dinner for all the models. Anything that could be done, I did it. What else could I do to help her? Keep in mind, During all of this she's still going to these political parties at that boathouse. A couple or few times she would come home and tell me that I was a topic of conversation where I was referred to as a AFRO-AMERICAN lover.

Now, after this, I started to think could they somehow be involved in my case a part OF this set-up or at least know about it. I just couldn't believe it. Who am I that all these politicians and wealthy men are somehow involved in framing me?! Then I started thinking that maybe it's not me, but my dad they are angry at thereby attacking me. I surely didn't know what was going on. I was like what do I do? My praying increased a thousand fold. I had no where to turn except look up towards heaven and cry out to Jesus. The uncertainty of everything became so bad that I decided to follow my FIANCEE to this one political party where many many people were going to attend without her knowing it. I parked a distance away from the party and waited for her to leave the party. When I eventually saw her leave the party and pass me by, I went to the party and asked for Tom Jackson. A man asked who I was and I said "Jack Ace, Sally Strawberry's ficancee. I want to talk to Tom Jackson." The man left and after a couple or few minutes, he came back with another man and said this is Tom Jackson. I told Tom Jackson who I was and asked if I could have a few words with him. So we walked outside and I said, "I need to find out what is going on with my case." Tom Jackson said, "Don't worry, it's all being worked out." Then I said, "But it's taking a long time. what's going on with it.?" Then Tom Jackson said, "these things take time. yours is a very major case with some very serious charges. But don't worry. It's all working out nicely. Everything is going to be OK." Then I said, "OK, sorry to bother you like this. but I needed to know something." and I left. Once again, as time went by, the pressure on my fiancee was getting worse by the ways I mentioned before or up above, and I still had no work and my case was still getting continued. Around this time, a major ruling was set forth by the judge and it was beneficial to me. Instead of me facing all the charges at one time, the judge severed or separated the charges so they can be tried individually.

Out of the 5 charges of arson, one was dropped because it was my neighbor's house. So I guess that since I had no vested interest in it and it didn't belong to me, that charge was dropped. So now I am facing 4 charges of arson. The judge made the house explosion a case by itself. The house on ORANGE STREET and my house on the lake was made into a case by itself. Last, he made the house that I was helping my worker to buy a case by itself and this will be the first charge of arson that I WILL GO TO trial on. So I was given a notice to re-appear to court for the first trial. This gave me a big relief for two reasons. One, I would be tried for only one count of arson and not 4 counts of arson with two to them carrying a mandatory of 5 year jail sentence each. Second, it gave me confirmation that all these wealthy men and politicians are really helping me and maybe they needed more time to find out who's behind all this. Once again, time went on and nothing really changed. My fiancee was being ripped apart with all this crazy pressure she was dealing with and I still couldn't get any work. As a matter of fact, the pressure was getting so worse we started arguing and fighting. She was getting exhausted physically and mentally whipped. I so wanted to help her but felt powerless. Then I started to fast trying to get some sort of miracle or for God to give her strength. She was truly being ripped apart. Once again, time went on and my case was getting continued, continued, continued! Then finally, I was at my trial. My lawyer told me it would be best to take the 5th amendment and not testify. So I did. I once tried to tell my lawyer about the things that were said in the interrogation room, he cut me off and said he didn't really want to hear that and that we must focus on the evidence against me. Supposedly the police officers claim to have all this evidence. But to this day, I still never seen any evidence. It wasn't at my trial. The only thing used at my trial was my worker's testimony, and the two officer's testimonies. So where was all this fire scene evidence?!! Also my lawyer at the trial never asked me to speak to my worker, nor did he even attempt to speak to my worker. For if he would have asked me to get him, I would have immediately went and got him and brought him over. Just like I did with my appeal lawyer. When my lawyer told me that we must focus on the evidence against me, I really thought there was some kind of fire evidence and it was being checked for fingerprints and examined in a laboratory or something.

BUT ONCE AGAIN, I STILL TO THIS DAY HAVEN'T SEEN ANY FIRE SCENE EVIDENCE.!!!! By the way, my worker has come into the office of my appeal lawyer and'taped a confession that his first testimony was false because he was coerced and threatened by the cops and District Attorney. Also soon after that taped confession, he has come back to court and got on the witness stand and testified that he was lying at the first trial and that I had nothing to do with any fraud or scam. My worker has even said that the D.A. called his mother and told her that if she didn't get my worker to court, he would arrest her and her daughter. To sum up, my worker was thinking that if he was to change his statement, he'll get charged by the F.B.I.., for all the arson charges, and for perjury, his mother would go to jail, and his sister would go to jail. I didn't know any of this was happening to him. My worker had a public defender representing him. Back to the trial. It was morning and they were doing the jury selection. I noticed a peculiar thing. There must have been a hundred court room security guards. They were standing around the entire room. I was thinking, Why in the world are there so many court security guards. Well as the trial proceeded and the jury selection was finished, they called the first witness. I think it was one of the arresting officers. The officers stated that I confessed to everything. I never said one word in that interrogating room. They never asked me one question. They made that entire thing up. From the moment when I was waiting in the waiting room of the police station and waiting for them to come to the police station and they walked in and told me to Get Up you are under arrest, I knew I had the right to remain silent, so I never said one word during the entire time I was with them. So my worker testifies and he won't look at me while testifying because I knew he felt bad about lying like that especially when all I ever did for years was help him out. So now the trial is over. The jury goes into another adjacent room for deliberations. I guess it was about 5 or 6 p.m. Well, we were waiting and then one of the ladies back by the Judge said, "Man, I wish the jury will 'hurry up. I'm ready to go home." So I guess about an hour later about 7 or 8 p.m. the jury comes back out. They read the verdict and it was guilty. The judge tells me to come up to a table to get a notice to re-appear to court for sentencing.

When I went up to that table to get the notice, the guy who handed me the notice was a court room security guard. As he handed me the notice and as I grabbed it he said, "Looks like you've been ripped off" and he smiles. I took the notice and went back to my seat. HOW COULD I BE GUILTY?! after all this time and waiting all this time. Now, I was completely confused and terrified. Then I realized all these politicians and wealthy men were burying me. I naturally file an appeal with a highly reputable lawyer but lost that appeal. This appeal lawyer was the one that when I was explaining the case, he asked me if I could get my worker to come in to his office so we could tape record him and I said sure. So I went and found him and brought him to my appeal lawyer and my appeal lawyer asked him some questions. All that time, he was being recorded. One of the questions was "Did Jack Ace have anything to do with the fire?" and my worker said, "NO." Well after that appointment, my attorney asked if I could get my worker to come into court and testify that he was lying at his original testimony at my trial. I said, "I'm not sure, but I will try. So, I left his office and went looking for him. I found him and asked him. He basically said "Jack Ace, I could go to jail for the rest of my life but I know it's the right thing to do. So I called my attorney and told him that he agreed to go back to court and testify to the truth. So another court date was set. My attorney, my worker, and I went to court. Three court officials grabbed my worker and told me to sit down. When I sat down, I couldn't See my worker. They had him surrounded at that witness stand. My worker point blank told everyone in court "Jack Ace had nothing to do with the fire at his house on Orange Street. My worker said he lied at the trial because he felt tricked. One of the conditions my worker told me that he would come back to testify and tell the truth was he wasn't going to say anything about how the cops were beating him and about how his mother and sister were threatned to be put in jail. He said that he would just say that he lied and I had nothing to do with the fire because he was afraid that the cops might go find him and hurt him or his mother, or his sister. Also, he didn't want the D.A. to put his mother or sister in jail. It took a lot of courage for him to come back like that. He did his best, He did the right thing. This was great and I was happy, but I thought it was strange was nobody asked him why did he lie at his first testimony. I mean isn't it the job of these law officials to find the truth and seek justice in any and every direction. For if they would had question my worker properly, then he would have stated all the ways he was being coerced and threatened, him and his family. My worker's public defender, my lawyer at the beginning of all this, my lawyer at this time, absolutely no one asked my worker what happened during his arrest and interrogation. They only asked questions around the false confession and that was it. I mean wouldn't it be a logical question to ask my worker, "Why did you lie?" I believe right then and there with that question, my case could have been blown open and completely turned around. My worker just coming back to court like he did and completely changing his statement like that was enough in itself for an immediate reversal of the conviction and break this case wide open. The judge rejected my worker's new testimony and upheld the conviction or verdict. So since I lost the appeal, my attorney referred me to another attorney. That new attorney filed for another appeal but we lost this appeal as well. Now I really thought, I'M REALLY ALONE!!

All the help that I thought I had on the outside of this thing were in fact burying me. So I decided to go to every law enforcement agency I could think of to tell them my case. First I went to the F.B.I. I explained the whole case to a lady and a man. They said they would review it and get back to me. I never heard back from them. I went to the State Attorney in the City of Gomorrah, our state's capital. After I explained the whole thing to him, he replied, "You sound like any other person that got convicted by someone else's testimony. So I figured I wasn't going to get any help there. Then I started thinking maybe the F.B.I. is thinking or feels the same way this Attorney General in City of Gomorrah. So I wasn't going to get any help there as well. I just couldn't believe this nightmare. I kept feeling I needed go higher up the legal system, but I didn't know where else to go. Then I decided if I make a big enough noise or rukus, then someone higher up the legal system would take notice and look into my case and put an end to this nightmare. I had already file a law suit against many defendants who were connected to my case, but I didn't serve anyone because my case was still getting continued every month. The defendants were all the insurance companies connected to this case, ABC Public Service, the police officers, the D.A., and the news people. The law in Sodom City states that all civil law suits must be filed one year from date of the knowledge of the offense. So I filed the lawsuits inside the one year time limit and they were just sitting there waiting to be served. BUT MY CASE NEVER GOT RESOLVED! just continued. So, I decided to serve all the defendants of my lawsuit and there were many. I even sued the bar association because I felt that someone or organization should have been overseeing these cases to make sure everyone is doing their job correctly and doing it well thereby true justice is served and no one gets falsely accused or convicted or jailed. For if there was such a person overseeing these trials and court proceedings. maybe they could ask questions that weren't asked by anyone in the court room that should have been asked.

So after I served all my defendants of my law suit, nothing happened. I reported to court once more and was taken into custody. I kissed my fiancee one last time and was taken away. I guess all those politicians and wealthy men won. I did everything I could do. They finally got my fiancee and got rid of me for 18 months which is half of a three year sentence. I was put into a place called SCP(Sodom County Prison). I was put into a place where there were many inmates doing life sentences. It was horrible. Toilets were lined up in a row maybe about 15 to 20 of them. There were no stalls or walls or anything for privacy, just open toilets. I saw no tissue paper for the toilets. There were a bunch of double metal bunk beds lined up on both sides of the room. After one night I was there, an inmate walked up to me and said, "I don't know who you are and you don't know me, but word is going around that they are going to shank you, probably when you are sleep at night." and he walked off. I immediately called my fiancee on the prison phone and said, "you gotta get me out of here. I don't feel safe. I think I'm in danger here." So my fiancee started calling around to see if I could be transferred and it worked. The next day, I was transferred to another facility. So after a week or two into my jail sentence, everybody started telling me "Don't worry, It snaps right back like a rubber band." All these inmates whom I have never met Started telling me this. Who has this kind of power? There's got to be about 2 or 3 thousand inmates in a facility and most of all of them in every direction were telling me this. I felt like I was in a horrible SCI-Fi movie or the Twilight Zone!!! The only thing I could figure was Whoever engineered all these inmates to tell me this must have been done by all these politicians and wealthy men that my fiancee was trying to keep happy the past 4 or 5 years. It was some kind of message to me that they were going to do my fiancee since I'm locked up and out the way.

I WAS CRUSHED!!! They did this just to torment and torture me mentally. Also, during my time in jail, I was striped search for about 4 months everyday because they knew I was a shy type. Another inmate felt sorry for me and told me, "You have to tell them, you are going to make me gay by making me *come* in here everyday and showing you my naked body." Well, I did it and it worked. They never stripped search me Again. There were a lot of scary fights and the guards would come in and take both participants and put Them in the hole. My fiancee visited me every single visiting day for my entire sentence. I had to call Her collect since I was on a prison phone and I called every single day I was in jail. Her phone bill must Had been 2 to 3 thousand dollars a month. I wrote letters to every single pastor and preacher thoughout the entire country trying to get some outside help. I even wrote letters to 4 or 5 talk shows on TV, such as Geraldo and Oprey Winfrey. When it came time For my probation hearing, which was the 12 months of me being in jail, prison officials told me to say I was guilty and they will release me out on probation. If I say I'm not guilty, they will think you have not learned your lesson and you aren't really rehabilitated and not release you out on probation. So I did as they told me to do and said I was guilty and they still denied my probation. So I had to serve the full 18 month sentence. I served the full 18 month sentence and my fiancee was there at the prison in the City of Gamorrah to pick me up when I was released. We were happy to see each other but I felt something was missing or wasn't there. We were both exhausted and maybe because we were so exhausted it took some of the magic away that we once had for each other. However, we were definitely happy that I had been released. So we went home. We did our best to pick up the pieces of what was left of our lives and start again, but the problems or attacks from her business doubled since the time before I went to jail.

And once again, I mysteriously couldn't get any work, so I was once again doing everything I could to help her. However, it wasn't enough. The magic we had started deteriorating we started arguing more and more. The pressure she was going through became too unbearable. So, SHE LEFT ME!! She simply disappeared. I came home one night and she wasn't home. I was alone now And waited for her to come home, but she never did. I even went to every bar and disco in the entire City of Sodom and all other surrounding areas hoping to see her out with friends so I could talk to Her. I was unsuccessful. Then after 6 or

7 months of doing this, I gave up on waiting for her and figured She wasn't coming back. So I really couldn't stay in the City of Sodom with just too many bad memories, so I decided to leave and make a new start at another place, a new city, and state. So I decided to go to Bethel, Isreal. I got down on my knees and said a prayer. I basically said, "Lord you saw everything that was done to me, take care of them all." Then I said "Amen." I got up and left for Bethel. A few Years later while I was in Bethel, Fire came down from the sky and wiped out the entire city of Sodom. THE ENTIRE CITY OF SODOM GONE!!!! My little brother was already living in Bethel, Isreal, so I stayed with him to get started or to get on my Feet so to speak. He had told me that he has so much work that he had to turn work away. So I thought I could handle his overflow only and establish a clientel of my own and get started living there. Under No condition, I wanted to disturb his normal customers, just his overflow that he has to turn away. Well I got there and started helping him with his current work load and all of a sudden, his normal, Regular, and overflow customers were pulling out or cancelling their jobs or work that they wanted my brother to do. I told my brother. "What In The World is going on? I come here to get some work from this great overload of work you had, but now we are just sitting here and looking at each other both unemployed with not a job in sight anywhere." He said "I don't know." Then I decided to run to the Mercy Seat. I found a small church

near to where I lived and started hitting the altars praying very diligently. God answered my prayers. I started getting work. However, I wasn't getting big projects. I was getting a lot of repair work or renovations. I changed many toilets in Bethel. At one time, I decided to go to another location further West to see if I can get some bigger projects. In this new location, contractors must be state licensed. If a contractor is not licensed, then that contractor can't do any projects. So I applied and passed all the tests, but when it came time to pass the criminal part of the application, I was denied. It was because of the arson charges and conviction I got back in the City of Sodom. I was denied. So I decided to go back to Bethel because I couldn't work in this new location. All the times I was in Bethel before and after this new location in the West, I was being attacked socially or when I went out socially. I've been out to many bars and discos growing up, so I know what is normal or usual or standard behavior is.

However the events that were happening to me in Bethel were so strange and bizarre, I had to conclude that a third party was involved in engineering these events against me. A few examples are One, I met this girl from Mongolia. She takes a mouthful of drink into her mouth and spits it all over me. I looked at the bartender and he looks at me. Then I looked at the bouncer and he didn't do anything. Then a customer next to me told me, "Dude, I saw what happened and I'll tell the owner of the bar."

So I just walked to the bathroom and try to clean or dry myself off and then went home. Another example was I was making eye contact with this girl and she gave me every sign to come over to say hi to her and meet her. So I did. When I said "Hi or Hello," she completely cursed me out saying some very bad words several times. All I could do was just walk away immediately. Another example was when this girl and I were clicking or getting along well, or at least I thought we were. We were laughing, joking, and conversating well and she says "You want to go?" and I said, "sure." We go outside and she says, "Let's go in my car. I have a new Lexus." and I said, "ok sure." So we get to her house and we walk in about 15 to 20 feet. She looks at me and says, "You see this beautiful mansion? Don't you wish you could have one of these?! Now, get out OF my house!" I was shocked and she looked scary. So I walked out immediately. I had no idea where I was at and had to walk miles to call a cab. It's a bad feeling to walk out of a house and not know what direction to walk in to get to your home.

Above are only a few examples of soooooooo many things or ways they were attacking my social life. I even went to a place far North of the country before I went back to Bethel thinking I need to get away from the enemy element I had in the City of Sodom. I need to get as far as I can because of these social and other attacks I was going through in Bethel. I was refused entry into this place far

North. The reason why was because when I reach this far North place border, two border officials completely emptied my truck in which there were many tools. Along with these tools, they found a small duffle bag of gun parts which belonged to my dad when he was a gun collector. My dad stopped this hobby and gave this bag of parts to me and that is why I had it. Well in this bag, along with other many parts, there were parts to an UZI. The prison official saw this and said to me, "You have an UZI." I said "Look at it. It is only a part to an UZI. "It is not a full UZI. Just parts." The border official put it back into the duffle bag. Then another border official asked me, "Do you have any cash?" and I said, "Yes" and they said, "How much?" and I said, "$15,000" and then they asked, "Where is it?" and I said, "on my front seat at the bottom of a Kleenex box." They went and got it. So after sitting there for about another 30 minutes, the border officials came back and gave me my cash back, took or seized my gun parts, and told me to go back to America. So I guess this place far North was no longer an option for me to live. That is actually the time I decided to go back to Bethel and look up my old clientel and start again.

Well, I'm back in Bethel still doing small jobs and not really getting anywhere in my social life or not getting any big jobs, still changing a lot of toilets. Also customers were stealing my tools off my jobsites and sabatoging or damaging my jobs when I wasn't there. Also, when I was in the new location out West, I had met this dentist that would trade services with me. I would do a job as an exchange for dental work. It started out ok, but my clamps were being stolen. So I decided I had better quit this deal set-up before things esculate. I had met this one girl in Bethel and we started to see each other or dating. She was from China. We started buying rental properties together. She would buy them and I would fix them up and rent them out. Then one day like all of a sudden all of the tenants were tearing them up and then leave owing back rent. I would go in there and fix them up again for free trying to help my girlfriend at that time, but it got worse and worse. I would still go in there and fix them up again. This happened about 10 times and once again I realized we were being attacked by a third party because this STUFF is just not normal. This girl from China and I started arguing from the pressure of all this and sorta split up, but remained friends. Well, I realized that these rental properties being torn up wasn't going to stop because it was a never ending cycle, so I decided to go to Vietnam to see the world, and winded up living in Cambodia teaching English. I first decided to go to Vietnam because I had met this Vietnam lady in Bethel and I took her out for dinner. She told me that there were many beautiful ladies in Vietnam and everything there was very cheap. Also, I always wanted to see the world, so I decided to go there first and I left. Now, I was on the other side of the world and I thought maybe just maybe I can live a nice peaceful life with no type of interference.

I was teaching as a profession and there were 100s and 100s of PRETTY ladies. I was getting paid cheap, but the cost of living was very low. I was like a upper-middle class person in a poor country. So I started teaching and the students loved me. They gave me parties in all levels. I taught elementary, high school, college, special groups, and the General of Cambodia and his soldiers. Teaching was great. As far as my social life, I started having some of the same problems like I had back in Bethel. I couldn't believe these PEOPLE followed me all the way to the other side of the world. I would show interest in someone, and the next thing I saw was 5 guys around her probably intimidating and scaring her. Now this someone that I had shown interest in had been sitting alone night after night for a couple of weeks. So like I said, I went over to talk with her and after a little while, I would have to go to the bathroom and so I went. I come back from the bathroom and she would be surrounded by guys. All I could do was just walk away. The very next night, she would be alone again sitting in the same spot. As a matter a fact, she would be there several days more and once again I make an attempt to speak to her. **We would talk** for a while and then I go buy a drink and I come back and once again, she is surrounded by guys. So I just walk away. Sometimes I try to go quicker trying to speed up the process of falling in love, but everyone knows you can't hurry love. I would meet them, buy them drinks, take them to dinner, and maybe go for motor bike ride around the city all in one night.

However, the second I am away from her, these guys would just come in like a stampede. This was bad enough, but the situation got worse. They, maybe the F.B.I., tried to assassinate me or kill me three times. One night I was on my motorbike getting ready to take off and as I was taking off, this car came straight at me. I sped up between two other cars and that car had to slam on his brakes to not hit the two cars that I went between. Then I drove out on the other side of the two cars that I sped to go in between. When I did this, the car put his car into reverse backs up and puts his car into Drive and started driving straight for me again. So I took off as fast as I could down the street. Well, this car starts to chase me. My heart sank and started racing at the same time. I was thinking, there is no way I can outrun a car and he's obviously trying to hit me. So I started zig-zagging everywhere. Anytime I could take a left or right as I was going full speed, I did it. Still he was getting closer and I knew I needed to go into some place where he couldn't fit, so I started looking while I was zig-zagging. Suddenly, I saw a place and it was a close call because the moment I drove into that narrow space, he was right there inches away. So I drove up about 10 feet and looked back. He just sat there and looked at me realizing the chase is over because he couldn't go any further. So he backed up and left. That was a truly terrifying experience especially when you are not ready for it. It just happens out of nowhere.

A second time where they, possible the F.B.I., tried to assassinate or kill me was when they set a trap for me and I went right into it. It was a miracle of God that I survived. I think the reason they set this unique trap for me was because they realize it would be too hard to try to just hit me with a car. What they had to do was to slow me down, so then they could hit me with a car. So one morning at about 2 or 3 a.m., I was going home with this girl in the back of me on my motorbike. As we were driving, I saw up ahead two individuals on their own motorbikes sitting in the center of an intersection of two streets. Well, naturally, I slowed down as I started to pass them and as I was passing them, my eyes were glued on them wondering what in the world are they doing just sitting here in the middle of an intersection at 2 or 3 a.m. Well, the moment when I was right upon them or right beside them, a car that was parked on the corner of the adjacent street must have had his engine running and in gear ready to just take off, because right when I was beside those two other guys with their motorbike, the car took off and hit me. Before I went down, I made eye contact with the driver of that car. He was a skinny Cambodian man with a F.B.I cap on. I'll never forget that. Well, the girl went flying, I went flying, my motorbike went flying. We were all sprawled out on the street. The car and the two motorbikes fled. The girl I was with was just laying there moaning and groaning in pain. I was in pain. My motorbike was about 10 feet away on its side. There was no one else in sight. So I started thinking. Oh My Goodness, I don't know where the hospital is or the police. There are no pay phones and you just can't dial 911. Everybody is asleep now even the police and the hospital. I don't even know how to get to the nearest hospital or police station. All I know is how to get home. So I decided to try to get her to my home and take care of her there until morning when everyone wakes up and everything opens up. So now I have to get myself up and get the motorbike up and see if it is still operable and then somehow get her on the motorbike and then go slowly home. So, I get to the motorbike and I'm hurting pretty bad. I pick it up and start it up and shift it in gear and make a circle around in the street to see if it's driveable.It seems fine. So I put down the kickstand and get off the motorbike to go get her. She's still moaning and groaning in pain and She looks so hurt. I remember thinking. Oh Lord, please don't let her die, Please Lord, Please Please!!! I don't know if she has broken anything or how close she is to death. I mean I'm not a doctor and I had heard that sometimes you shouldn't jackknife a patient if they are hurt a certain way. But still, I had toget her to my house because we just can't sit in the street all night. So, I raised her shoulders up and put my arm under her legs and brought her to the motorbike and sat her towards the front of the bike where I can sit behind her. I thought I could better hold her in front of me while going home. Well I get her home and get her into bed and start trying to clean her up. Oh My Goodness, it was so terrible.

Well after about an hour, she wakes up and says she has to go home now. I tried telling her to rest and that she is very hurt, but she wouldn't listen. She says you don't understand. I must go now or my mom will kill me. So I backed off and open the door for her so she can leave. When she walked out the door and went about 6 to 8 feet, she completely collapses. I dash over to her and once again pick her up and bring her back into my place and put her back in bed. She is still insisting that she has to go home now. So I tried feeding her cake and giving her coke to try to give her energy, so she won't pass out again. The cake has sugar and the coke has sugar and caffeine. I tell her just eat a few bites and drink some coke before you try again, because you need energy. You are very weak. So she ate a little cake and drank some coke and she tried again. This time, I stood right next to her until she went out into the front of my place and I put her on motorbike taxi. I told the motorbike taxi guy to watch her close, she is very sick and weak. He said ok and they took off. In the meantime during all that, my real pain started to set in. I must have been in some sort of shock at my initial injury because it didn't hurt that much. However, it really started hurting and I was like limping for the next 6 months trying to recover from that injury. A third time when I felt like an attempt on my life was going down, was when I was sitting in the local pub. Well, as I was sitting there, two food court guards came up to me and one sat on the right of me about 5 feet away and the other sat on the left of me about 5 feet away. Well, they kept staring at me like something was going to go down, for I have been there in that seat a thousand times and they have never done this.Then, all of a sudden this little girl runs up and sits beside me. She wasn't really talking to me or anything, just sitting down there. Then the guards jump up and ran up to that little girl and made her go away. Now, I have had many people, male, female, young, and old sit beside me in that same spot and they have never worried or got up and ran over to me and make them leave.

Then all of a sudden, I got this premonition of two guys running up shooting at me, so I got up and left immediately. After I got about 10 feet away, the same two guards who were trying to make that little girl leave, walked away as well, So that little girl was the only one left sitting there where I was at, no guards or me. So as you can see, I was even having many problems on the other side of the world. So back to the driver who had that F.B.I. cap on. I remember thinking.Is it possible the F.B.I. are working with someone to try to have me killed by making it look like an accident. I guess looking at it in a big picture, it would be very acceptable to say I died in a car accident because I was drinking to much. Well after all this, you can just imagine how careful and alert I was in doing everything I was doing. So where do I go now? I guess the only other place is the moon. Lol Do you think they can get to me on the moon?

Lol So as of today, I'm still single recovering from brain surgery. Going back to the trial and charges of this book, what do you think? Am I guilty or innocent? You are the jury now. Did I do them all? Did I do some of them? Did the cops do some of them? Did they do all of them? Did they do my neighbor's house on the lake because they made a mistake and was one house off? My neighbor and I shared the same walk-way, so it can very easily be confused who the owner of each house was. You truly have all the facts and the evidence up above. Now you can make a sound and fair and impartial verdict or judgement. I never got to say a single word in my behalf through this entire ordeal. This book you are reading are my words finally. So many things has happened, unjust things. I just had to get my story out.

Finally I say something from my mouth for all the world to hear. I'm innocent of everything. I was set-up, convicted, buried, and demonized. In the end, all I have is Jesus, and **it** is said, "a man on his knees before God can take on the world."

At times, it has felt like I am taking on the world. Well, that's all I have been doing the last 30 years when all this started, Praying and Fasting. I do believe I'm only breathing today only because of God's grace and tender mercies. I'm grateful that with all these storms of life,God has brought me through it. I pray 5 or 6 times a day.

Thank you Jesus. PTL

A gain back to the my criminal case or trial. I never got to say one word and everyone the police came In contact with surrounding my case were frightened, intimidated, and traumatized. I don't care who You are. If two police officers come at you screaming and shouting and hitting you, you will be scared, And feel intimidated. My fiancee and my worker were terrified at these psycho police officers and then Go into a big courtroom with all these men with suits trying to put you away in jail for the rest of your Life, ABSOLUTELY!! It was all very scary. So let's see if we can group all the things wrong with this trial. One, the police officers are lying on the record, document proof. If one officer says one thing and the other officer says something else or differently on the exact question, then who is lying?!

They were both lying because I never said nothing. TRUTH AND JUSTICE DEMANDS THAT THEY MUST HAVE THE SAME ANSWER TO ANY QUESTION!!!! They never asked me one question in that interrogating room. Also if I did say all these things, why didn't they get me to sign a confession like they did with my worker. They straight up lied, committed perjury about ten counts each. Their entire testimony was made up. Second, the D.A. threatening my worker with federal time if **he** were to change his testimony. The D.A. threatening to put his mother and sister in jail. Yep, my worker was truly traumatized and had no choice, but to stick to his original false coerced statement. Third, I should have testified, but my lawyer told me that it would be best not to. Fourth, why didn't my lawyer question my worker? Or why didn't he ask me to bring my worker in to his office just like my appeal lawyer did and then question him. Also why didn't the judge question my worker, ANYONE!! I look back at all this and just shake my head. I certainly was na'ive and innocent in every sense of the word. I also certainly have no more faith in our justice system. All they had to do was just say "Did anyone hurt you or scare you, or make you say anything that is not true? That question would have Blown this case wide open turn the situation completely around, because my worker would have then felt safe Thinking they were on his side and that he don't have to be so scared of the psycho cops and he then Would have spoken the truth. My worker was man-handled roughly, hit, threanten, and his family threatened all the way from the Police officers to the D.A. He is also thinking the F.B.I. are lurking somewhere nearby just ready to come In and be far more worse than the cops beating him.

Since I have been through all this, I have been taking notice through the years of convictions of different crimes being reversed. A man spends 20 something years in jail and Because of the new technology of D.N.A., it proves his innocence. Another man spends 17 years in jail And once again, because of new technology, it proved that a fingerprint was not his, so he is immediately released. All I got to say is That something must be done. You just can't put a person away for many years and then realize it was A mistake. That is simply horrible.

I have one last thought that is certainly unthinkable with my case. Let's step back and look at the very Big general picture of everything I have said in this book. Could it be possible, that everything was a Complete set up all the way from the first event. The house explosion on Banana Street to the moment I Came back to America form Cambodia. The things that happen very ODD OR STRANGE things certainly could suggest so. The explosion, all the fires, fire scene evidence that I have never saw to this day, the charges be divided up, my lawyer, the jury being rigged, my trial being rigged, my appeals being denied, My planned murder in that first facility where I should have not been because I didn't have a violent Charge and that place was full of lifers, an entire prison telling me it will snap back like a rubber band at another facility, the three murder attempts on my life in Cambodia, many tools stolen from me on my jobs, my jobs being damaged or destroyed, Etc. etc.

In the beginning or towards the beginning of all these events, I had been formulating a theory that ABC Public

Service was behind all this because after the explosion, many people in the neighborhood were suing ABC Public Service saying they were hurt or injured. Therefore, if they were to frame me or set me up by having my properties burn down and I get convicted, ABC Public Service would be released from paying all those lawsuits off. However, as of today, with so many things that has happened and all this time that has passed, I must say that this theory has to be changed.

My next theory as of today is could it be possible that a very rich evil tycoon who has ties to or is an affiliate to the insurance industry has dirty cops and dirty FBI agents working for him/her? We are talking About thirty years now. Someone who is very prejudice or racist? Has the resources to engineer anything. My fiancée and I just wanted to get married and have little family. We weren't hurting anyone. She was working hard and I was working hard for our dream. However, they wanted her to be a madame of all the beautiful girls in the City of Sodom and have her and her models at their disposal and get rid of me. I guess they thought that if they put me in jail too long, my fiancée would be too devastated and might fold up her business. So they had to put me away just for a little while like 18 months and that would be enough to make her get rid of me. But they never never never knew of the great love we had and magic we had that it even can endure a prison sentence that they so conveniently put on me on us.

You have read my book above. Who has this kind of power. Basically, do anything they want, even play with me/us like a toy and get away with it. Well all I know is that I'm going to stay on my knees before the Lord And put it all into God's hands like I always do. I say "LORD, I GIVE IT TO YOU.DO AS YOU SEE FIT."

THE END

ABOUT THE AUTHOR

He's just an average guy working hard for the American dream, a wife and family.

Printed in the United States
By Bookmasters